# LOOK INSIDE

# A ROMAN VILLA

**Richard Dargie**
**Illustrated by Adam Hook**

HODDER
Wayland

an imprint of Hodder Children's Books

**Editor:** Jason Hook
**Designer:** Danny McBride

First published in Great Britain in 2000
by Wayland Publishers Ltd
This paperback edition published in 2002 by
Hodder Wayland, an imprint of Hodder Children's Books
© Hodder Wayland 2000

**British Library Cataloguing in Publication Data**
Dargie, Richard
   A Roman Villa. – (Look inside)
   1. Dwellings – Rome – Juvenile literature 2. Rome –
   Social life and customs – Juvenile literature 3. Rome –
   Civilization – Juvenile literature
   I. Title II. Hook, Adam
   937.6

ISBN 0 7502 2682 X

Production Controller: Carol Titchener
Colour reproduction by Page Turn, Hove, England
Printed and bound in Hong Kong

**Cover Pictures:** A fresco showing a family offering sacrifices to the gods (centre); a household god or lar (top-right); a hairpin (bottom-left); a bronze cooking skillet (bottom-right).

**Picture Acknowledgements.** The publishers would like to thank the following for permission to publish their pictures:
(l = left, r = right, t = top, b = bottom, c = centre)
AKG–London 10b, 26t, 27t, /Erich Lessing 6t, 15t, 18b, 21b, 24b, 29r, /Gilles Mermet 12b, 17b, 21t; Ancient Art & Architecture Collection 5t, 7c, 11b, 24t, /Brian Wilson 19b; Bridgeman Art Library /Villa dei Misteri, Pompeii *cover*, /John Bethell 4b, /Lauros–Giraudon 16t, /Santa Costanza, Rome 17t, /Index 19t, /British Museum 20t, /Museo della Civilta Romana, Rome, Italy 22t, /Ashmolean Museum, Oxford 25b, 26b, /Villa Romana del Casale, Piazza Armerina, Sicily 29l; British Museum, London *cover* tr, bl, br, 5b, 7b, 10t, 13t, 14t, 15b, 16bl, 18c, 18t, 28t; Colchester Museum 23b; e.t.archives 4t, 7t, 8–9t, 9b, 9c, 12t, 15c, 22b, 23t, 25t; Wayland Publishers 16br, 19c; Werner Forman Archive 11t, /J. Paul Getty Museum, Malibu 13b.
All artwork is by Adam Hook.
All quotes are credited on page 31.

KEY 6

SKILLET 18

AMPHORA 16

SCRUBBING BRUSH 14

# CONTENTS

VILLA 4

LAR 10

HAIRPIN 12

LYRE 22

STRIGIL 28

GLOSSARY 30

FURTHER
READING 31

INDEX 32

HELMET 26

SILVER DISH 20

MOSAIC 8

PUPPET 24

# VILLA

## A MAGNIFICENT HOME

The hot midday sun beats down on the red tiles of the villa roof. The white marble columns of the *colonnade* give shelter from the heat and the bright sunlight. A Roman senator and his family sit in the cool shade. They look out on the villa gardens and listen to the water bubbling in the fountains.

▲ A painting of a Roman villa built in AD 45.

*'I built this villa and it's fit for a god. It's got four dining rooms, twenty bedrooms, two marble colonnades and enough guest rooms for all of my friends.'* [1]

Many rich Roman families had large villas on their estates in the Italian countryside. The Romans also built villas in the countries they conquered such as Spain and England.

◄ Emperor Hadrian had this villa built near Rome, in AD 120.

Villas were first built on the hills overlooking Rome. Each summer, rich families left Rome when the city streets and drains became too smelly. They spent the hot summer months on their villa estates. Villas were magnificent houses, which were large and cool. They were usually surrounded by gardens with pools, fountains and marble statues.

The villa lay at the heart of a large working estate, with orchards, farms and forests. There were stables and barns, and sometimes a mill. Crops such as olives were harvested and stored, then sold in the city.

▲ You can find out where all our quotes come from by looking on page 31.

HOW TO RUN A VILLA

'The villa should be in three parts – the house where the family live, a farmhouse and a storehouse.' 2

◀ An ancient mosaic showing workers on a Roman villa estate.

The famous writer Pliny had a villa on the coast near Rome. Like most rich Romans, he visited his villa only in the summer. For the rest of the year, only the owner's slaves lived on the estate. Pliny proudly described his villa in letters to his friends, like the one below.

*'I am so fond of my villa at Laurentium. It is charming, with views of the sea, the shoreline and the distant mountains.'* 3

Some slaves on the villa estate were well educated, and were trusted by their master to run the estate for him. They were placed in charge of hundreds of ordinary slaves who served in the villa and worked in the fields.

▲ A bronze jar in the shape of a young slave taking a nap.

# KEY

## SLAVES AND SECURITY

'Get up! Get this whole area swept before the master's friends begin to arrive! Then get this hound watered and fed!' The *atriensis*, or doorkeeper, wakes the slave who has slept across the villa's main entrance all night. Then he takes a bronze key from his belt and unlocks the door to the *atrium*, or courtyard.

▲ A Roman lock and key, made out of bronze.

To keep out burglars, Roman villas had very few windows and only one main door. This was guarded day and night by a trusted slave called the atriensis. He carried keys and sometimes had a large guard dog at his side.

'The slaves who oversee the other slaves should have their rooms next to the cubicles where the common slaves live, so that they can keep an eye on everyone coming and going. The slave in charge of the atrium should also have a small room there.' [4]

The *cellarius*, or cellarman, was another slave who carried keys on his belt. He was in charge of the pantries and wine cellars built beneath the villa. Important slaves like the doorkeeper and cellarman had their own slaves to help them with their work.

◀ The doorkeeper wakes a sleeping slave.

▶ Villas were often guarded by large dogs called mastiffs.

Some lucky slaves had quite pleasant jobs in the villa. The *cubicularii* slaves served in the living rooms. Other slaves worked in the kitchens and bakehouse. The *focarius* slave had the job of keeping the fires and ovens alight.

'Make sure your slaves are treated well by the overseers. Check the quality of their food and drink by tasting it yourself. Also check their clothing and footwear.' 5

◀ A Roman carving showing a gang of chained slaves on a treadwheel.

'Common slaves' had tough jobs on the estate. The lowest ranked were chained together and ordered about by an overseer called the *silentarius*. Some of them spent their day simply walking on the spot to turn giant treadwheels. These powered the estate's cornmill and pumped water to the fountains.

◀ A slave's identity tag.

Common slaves wore a metal identity tag, and were beaten if they were caught running away. Household slaves were usually treated well and could win their freedom by giving good service. Freed slaves wore a different type of tag.

'Make sure you inspect your field slaves to see they are properly shackled and guarded. Keep them in an underground prison with narrow windows that cannot be reached from the ground.' 6

# MOSAIC

## DECORATING THE VILLA

'One more red marble will do it, and six weeks of work will be over.' The master craftsman selects a small piece of stone from his various boxes, and fits it into place. The mosaic pattern is complete. The face of a monster called a Minotaur, created from thousands of brightly coloured fragments, stares up from the floor.

*'We think ourselves poor if our villa walls are not resplendent with large and costly mirrors, or mosaics of African stone, or paintings, and if our swimming pools are not lined with marble.'* 7

▶ A painter's blocks of colour, preserved in Pompeii in the first century BC.

Rich Romans paid a fortune to decorate their villas. The most famous decoration was the mosaic, where coloured pieces were carefully arranged to form a picture.

◀ A craftsman completes work on the villa's mosaic floor.

Villa walls were built in red brick, and then beautifully decorated. The brick was hidden beneath a thick layer of plaster called stucco. Craftsmen then used a mixture of paint and beeswax to create pictures of animals, monsters or gods. Pictures called frescoes were painted on the plaster while it was still wet. It took great skill to paint in this way, and artists were richly rewarded.

The villa had a number of public rooms, where the owner met his friends and clients. He wanted to impress them, so these rooms were covered with mosaics and paintings. The private family rooms, though, were very plainly decorated.

*'A man who holds government office should build a lofty entrance, a spacious courtyard, a broad garden and a library, so that his villa looks suitable for a man of his importance.'* 8

*'Make sure you have a contract with workmen or they will do less work than you wish but charge you twice as much.'* 9

▲ Paints from all over the Empire were imported to decorate villas.

The Romans liked to create illusions with their villa paintings. The walls of rooms near the gardens were often decorated with fake windows showing 'garden scenes'.

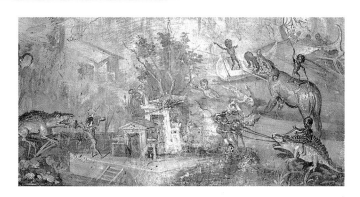

▲ This fresco shows children in Egypt playing with elephants and crocodiles in the River Nile.

In AD 79, a volcano in southern Italy called Vesuvius erupted. A deep flow of lava engulfed the nearby city of Pompeii, and completely covered the many villas built around the volcano. The lava preserved these villas and their beautiful decorations. They were rediscovered hundreds of years later, in almost perfect condition.

◄ This mosaic shows a panther stalking some birds as they drink in a villa fountain.

## GODS AND GHOSTS

The senator and his wife watch in silence, as their son reads a prayer. They place some flowers and scraps of food on a tray and hand it to a slave. She walks slowly to a shrine, and places the offering before the small, bronze statue of a household god.

▶ A holy biscuit called *libum* was offered to images of lares like this one.

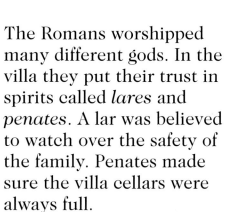

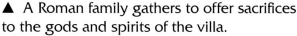
▲ A Roman family gathers to offer sacrifices to the gods and spirits of the villa.

The Romans worshipped many different gods. In the villa they put their trust in spirits called *lares* and *penates*. A lar was believed to watch over the safety of the family. Penates made sure the villa cellars were always full.

Some rooms in the villa contained a shrine called a *lararium*. Here the family placed fresh flowers, or food such as corn, for the gods and ghosts of the villa. The Romans believed it was very bad luck to forget to honour these spirits.

'The household ghosts ask for very little. They value your prayers more than a costly gift. A sprinkling of corn grains, some salt, or bread soaked in wine is enough.' [10]

Many villas had an altar where small animals were sacrificed to the gods by a priest. He believed he could see into the future by examining the entrails of these animals. It was thought to be a good omen if the entrails were healthy.

Some villas had special shrines where the family worshipped the spirits of their ancestors. Pieces of skin and hair from dead relatives were stored there. Some shrines also contained busts of these ancestors sculpted out of clay.

◄ Busts of dead relatives lined up at a family shrine in Pompeii.

A shrine was often found on the wall near the main doorway of the villa. This was dedicated to Vesta, the goddess of the hearth. She was believed to watch over households and families. She also made sure that mischievous spirits behaved themselves.

When a boy shaved for the first time, the hair from his chin was placed in one of the villa shrines. It was believed that the spirits would then protect him.

► A lararium from Pompeii. Snakes were thought to be sacred animals.

# HAIRPIN

## MIRRORS AND MAKE-UP

While the mistress admires her new hairstyle in a mirror, a slave mixes mercury and other metals to make a bright silver eyeshadow. This is skilled work. One drop too many and her mistress might be poisoned by the mercury!

▼ Golden rings and earrings from the first century AD.

◀ A necklace found in the grave of a Roman woman.

The mistress of the villa had several chamber slaves. The *cestellatrix* slave helped her to choose her jewellery for the day. She carried several *speculae*, or mirrors, made from brightly polished silver. Her mistress used these to admire her jewellery and make-up.

*'Nowadays even humble women go to the theatre and the games with their hair crimped and covered in semi-precious stones.'* 12

Rich Roman women were expected to dress simply in the family villa. But during festivals and holidays, they dressed to show off their wealth. Chamber slaves made new clothes for their mistress and helped her to dress.

▲ A mosaic of a slave holding out a mirror, so the mistress can arrange her hair.

▶ A beautiful Roman hairpin.

A good chamber slave knew how to create make-up. The Romans made lipstick from crushed moss. Coloured chalk, oils from sea creatures, and poisonous metals such as mercury were also used in make-up.

Perfumes from across the Empire ended up in the villas of Italy. Rich women prized sandalwood and frankincense, which were fragrances from Indian and Arabian trees.

*'A woman should wear no more cosmetics than her beauty needs and her good sense allows.'* 13

◀ Hairpins carved from bone and silver in the shape of the goddesses Fortunata (left) and Venus (right).

*'I saw Lollina Paulina at a banquet, covered with emeralds and pearls and shining all over her head and fingers; the total value was more than 40 million sesterces.'* 14

▶ A bone hairpin showing a woman's elaborate hairstyle.

A slave called the *calamistera* crimped her mistress's hair using hot, metal curling tongs. She styled it into piles and coils held up with beautiful hairpins. She also used tweezers to pluck out unwanted facial hair. Sometimes, her mistress might ask to wear one of her blonde or red wigs – which were made out of hair cut from the heads of foreign slaves.

▶ A Roman mistress selects her best jewellery for the day.

# SCRUBBING BRUSH

## THE LAUNDRY

'Pour in more urine!' shouts the overseer. A new batch of cloth has arrived at the villa laundry. Now the slaves prepare it for making into clothes. One woman pours urine into a tin bath. Her partner turns up her nose as she treads the urine into the cloth.

▶ Two slaves prepare new cloth by treading it in a tub of urine.

▲ Scrubbing brushes were used to prepare cloth. This brush was used in Roman Britain over 1,800 years ago.

Large villa estates had a laundry in which cloth was prepared. It was first washed and stiffened with urine. This was collected in pots left outside the villa doors. The stiffened cloth was scrubbed, then bleached using burning sulphur. Finally it was flattened in a huge clothes press. The skin of laundry slaves was covered in sores, caused by ammonia in the urine. Those in the bleaching room coughed constantly, because sulphur fumes burned their lungs.

Slaves also washed and pressed the family's clothes. By spitting mouthfuls of water on cloth before ironing, they achieved the effect of a modern steam-iron.

◀ Men wearing the traditional heavy, woollen toga.

The rich family who owned the villa wore clothes made from fine wools. On special occasions they wore silk. Slaves wore tunics made from coarser wool. The villa was very self-sufficient. Wool for cloth came from animals on the villa estate, and clothes were made by female slaves.

'As for wool, the softest is produced around Modena. The coarser wools, worn by slaves and in most Roman homes, comes from Liguria. Silk is bought in from Arabia and Egypt.' 16

▲ This villa painting shows the rich, thick cloth worn by wealthy women.

The long, heavy toga worn by men was often considered a nuisance. Laws were passed to force men to wear it. In AD 397 the Emperor Honorius banned men from wearing trousers as these were 'barbarian' clothes. There was also a law ordering Roman women to cover their hair in public.

◀ Women wore gowns and shawls pinned with gold brooches like this one.

# AMPHORA

## FARMING THE ESTATE

'Keep that basket steady!' shouts a slave from his perch in an olive tree. Balancing on a ladder, he snips the fruit with iron shears, and it falls to his partner below. It is September, time for harvesting the estate's orchards and vineyards.

▶ Slaves gather fruit in a wicker basket.

Many slaves worked on the villa estate, which produced all sorts of goods. Wheat was grown for the villa's bread. There were often beehives on the estate, as honey was used a lot in Roman cooking. Some slaves worked at the *cochlearia*. These were the farms where they bred edible snails!

*'Plant your orchard in a sloping place where the watery manure can flow and seep down, for vegetables and fruit trees thrive on nutrients of this sort.'* [17]

▶ Grapes were the main crop on most villa estates.

▶ Wine and olive oil were stored in special clay jugs called amphorae.

*'Store the villa's wine over the smoke house, for wines age more rapidly when they are matured by a certain kind of smoke.'* [18]

Olives and grapes from the villa estate were turned into oil and wine. This was then sold in the city. The Romans had specially shaped containers called amphorae which were used to transport and store these precious substances.

Wine was served with every meal in the villa. Even young children were given watered down wine to drink. Wine was also traded across the Roman Empire. The best was said to come from Spain and the Lebanon.

The Romans made wines in four colours: red, white, yellow and black. They believed that the secret of wine-making had been discovered by Bacchus, the god of drinking.

▲ Slaves bring a cartload of grapes to the villa wine-press.

'There should be two dungpits by the villa farmhouse. Store your fresh dung in one for a year or two, and haul out the old dung from the other one as you need it.' 19

'Take great care when your slaves are pouring wine into the vats. Otherwise they will syphon off some of the good wine for their own secret use.' 20

After being trodden, grapes were squeezed in a wooden press. This was done three times. The owner and his family drank the best wine, made from the first pressing. Slaves drank the poorest wine, from the third pressing. Wine was stored in big vats in cool cellars. Some wines needed fifteen years in storage before they were ready to drink.

▶ Slaves press the harvested grapes by trampling on them.

# SKILLET

## IN THE KITCHEN

'Pour more blood into the skillet and chop up some of that calf brain! That's the way Antoninus likes it!' The chef is making *tomasculum*, a special kind of meat pudding. It will be served at a banquet to celebrate the freeing of one of the senior slaves.

▶ Roman chefs cooked food over gridirons, like this one found in England.

◀ A Roman bronze skillet found in England.

*'The salvers were laden with stuffed roast dormice sprinkled with honey and poppy seeds. The sausages were smoking on a silver gridiron with sliced damsons and pomegranates.'* [21]

Kitchen slaves were the luckiest on the villa estate, and the best fed. They had to prepare food for the owner and his family four times a day. Breakfast, 'elevenses' and lunch were usually very simple meals. The Romans liked to save room for an enormous dinner, or *coena*, in the late evening.

The centre of the kitchen was the butcher's block, where the chef prepared all his recipes. Hams and other meats were hung from the kitchen ceiling to cure and preserve them. The Romans had no fridges so they often hung up meat in a sausage-skin called a *botulus*.

▶ Kitchen slaves chopping food and sifting flour.

◀ Fish were a popular mosaic pattern. Many villas had fishponds for a supply of fresh fish.

◀ Lentils were a large part of a slave's diet.

Typical cooking ingredients included lentils, beans, olives and curdled milk. Every kitchen also had at least one amphora of garum. This was a strong sauce made from fish entrails and blood. The Romans used it to flavour their favourite meals.

'Anthemius is sick fed up with eating lentils.' 23

◀ Carved serpents were worn as bracelets by chefs.

Cleanliness was important in the villa kitchen. Chefs often wore bracelets shaped like serpents. This was a tribute to Anguis, the snake-like god of cleanliness and good health.

'Feed your slaves well but only on simple foods. If you give them a taste for rich food, they will eat their way through your storehouse.' 24

Only properly trained slaves were allowed to work in the busy villa kitchen. Villa owners paid large sums of money to buy a skilled chef at the local slave market.

# SILVER DISH

## THE BANQUET

The *praegustator*, or food-taster, carries in a roast flamingo set on a magnificent silver dish. He slices a sliver of meat and tastes it, to check it is not poisoned. He nods and smiles. The banquet can begin. The *scissor* slave steps forward and starts to carve the bird.

▶ A Roman silver banqueting dish found at Mildenhall in Suffolk, England.

Banquets were held regularly at the villa. When the guests arrived, they filled their goblets from a large open bowl of wine called a *crater*. Then they reclined on one of the couches in the dining room.

'Each one of the slaves in the household sang as they did their labours. You would have thought you were at a theatre rather than in the dining room of a gentleman's house.' [25]

A slave called the *scissor* announced each dish, carved it, then served the guests. Another slave, the *scurra*, had the job of flattering the diners. He also announced toasts and made sure the guests behaved.

◀ A slave serves flamingo dressed with oysters and radishes.

Banquets were a good opportunity for the owners of the villa to show off their wealth. At one banquet, the host changed into a different set of expensive clothes between each of the thirteen courses.

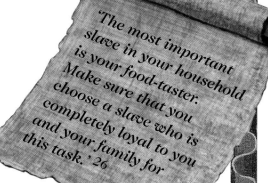

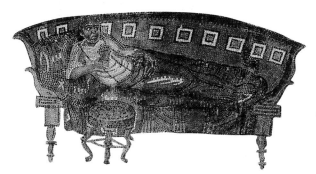

◄ Guests reclined on couches to dine.

After eating, diners belched as a mark of respect to the host. Banquets had many courses, and it was also normal behaviour for diners to 'disgorge', or vomit, one course to make room for the next.

'One slave mops up the disgorged food, another crouches beneath the table and gathers up the leftovers of the drunken guests. Another skilfully carves the expensive game birds.' 27

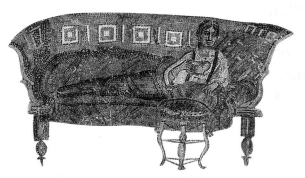

Throughout the banquet, slaves looked after the diners. Some massaged their feet and cut their toenails. Others handed out treats such as the eggs of geese and thrushes. At the end of the meal, slaves poured water over the guests' hands and cleaned their fingernails.

▶ Slaves at a banquet. One is helping a diner to disgorge his meal.

# LYRE

## ENTERTAINING THE GUESTS

A bell rings to signal the end of the feasting. The atriensis opens the villa door and lets in a troupe of Greek entertainers. They carry in lyres, cymbals and bagpipes and begin to tune up. Some African dancing girls practise their steps, while they wait for the guests to walk through from the dining room.

▶ A modern reconstruction of a Roman lyre, a stringed instrument made with the shell of a tortoise.

*'It is best to leave banquets early before the lyre-player drinks too much and starts to sing too loud.'* [28]

The early Romans were not known for their interest in music. After their legions conquered Greece in 150 BC, however, it became fashionable to listen to Greek music.

When a family entertained friends in their villa, Greek slaves played music for the guests. Slaves not only played at banquets but also at religious ceremonies. Here they were expected to play as loudly as possible to drown out any noises that might bring bad luck.

◀ A fresco from a villa in Pompeii, showing the god Pan playing a lyre.

After dinner, there was music, dancing, reciting of poetry and gambling. Some guests preferred to walk outside and smell the flowers. The gardens were lit by lanterns and torches. Small sparkling discs called *oscillae* were hung from the trees to catch and reflect the moonlight.

◀ An educated slave recites a poem.

◀ An entertainer plays the tambourine.

Villa owners showed off their most educated slaves after a banquet. It was a sign of wealth to have your own poets who composed and recited flattering songs about their master.

*'When I sup with my wife or a few close friends, a book is read or there is a dramatic reading from a comedy, or music. Then I walk and discuss matters with some of my domestic slaves who are learned men.' 30*

▶ A slave serves snacks to guests arriving after dinner.

▶ A guest enjoys the entertainment.

Many guests were expected to dine elsewhere. They were invited to the villa only for the after-dinner entertainments. Slaves served them with wine and *placentae*, which were small cakes of wheat, cheese and honey.

# PUPPET

## GROWING UP

'Please hand that puppet to me, young master,' pleads the slave. 'You know you should be studying, not playing. Your tutor will return to the villa tomorrow. You know that I, your poor *paedagogus*, will be beaten if you do not complete your reading and writing exercises.'

▶ Children played with clay puppets, like this one of a Roman soldier.

▲ Young children playing in the villa courtyard.

Children from rich families were taught in the home. Tutors for different subjects came to the villa to instruct them. The paedagogus was the slave placed in charge of the children. He also helped with their studies.

The paedagogus was responsible for watching over the child in his care at all times. It was seen as his fault if the child misbehaved. If his pupil fell behind in his studies, or got into trouble, it was the slave who was punished and beaten.

*'Cato taught his son to read, even though he had a slave who was a teacher. However Cato did not think it was right ... so he taught his son reading, law, athletics, horse-riding and how to fight in armour.'* [31]

◀ A girl with a wax tablet and stylus.

*'You accursed schoolteacher! What right do you have to disturb us with your savage threats and beatings? Let your pupils go!'* 33

Villa children learned to write in Latin or Greek using a tablet of soft wax. They etched their letters on the wax using a sharp needle or *stylus*. Children practised for hours in the shade of the colonnade, keeping the wax out of the sunlight so that it would not melt.

Young boys had to wear a special toga which had a purple hem. On their sixteenth birthday, a ceremony was held in the villa for the family gods. Then the boy was allowed to wear the white toga of a man.

◀ These bullae, or lucky charms, were worn by Roman children. Only freeborn children, not slaves, could wear them.

Roman children wore good-luck charms called *bullae* around their necks, to ward off evil spirits. When they became adults, the charms were placed in a lararium, so that the gods would continue to keep their owners safe.

# HELMET

## SCHOOL FOR GLADIATORS

'Never slash about wildly with your sword!' growls the scarred, old gladiator. 'Your enemy will see a weak point, and you'll soon be dead. Always thrust forward with the point of the sword!' He demonstrates the move with his wooden baton, as the trainee gladiator looks on.

'Emperor Hadrian forbids any master to sell one of his slaves to a trainer of gladiators without good reason. Thus, only suitable and skilled men will be seen in the arena.' 34

▶ The face and head of a gladiator were protected by this helmet of bronze and iron.

Gladiators fought to entertain thousands of spectators at public games. These were held in amphitheatres in the main cities. Most gladiators were trained at special schools on the villa estates of powerful Roman senators. Many of these estates were in Campania, in the countryside south of Rome.

◀ A model of a gladiator with a heavy, oblong shield and a short, iron sword.

Some villa owners in Campania ran their gladiator schools as a business. They bought prisoners of war who were on sale at the slave markets in Rome. These prisoners were instructed by a retired gladiator at a training camp on the villa estate. The owner then made money by betting on his fighters when they appeared in the arena.

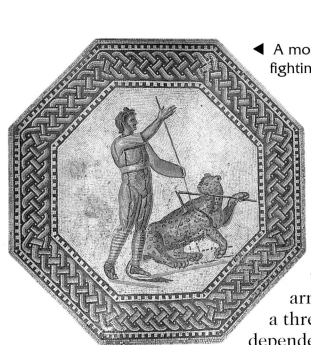

◄ A mosaic of a gladiator fighting a panther.

There were four main types of gladiator. The Mirmillo and Samnite wore armour. The Retarius had no armour, but used a weighted net and a three-pointed trident. The Thracian depended on a curved sword and his speed.

*'The afternoon combats are pure murder. The gladiators have no armour. All of their bodies are exposed to the sword and each lunge strikes home. The outcome for the fighters is death.'* 36

A skilled gladiator might earn a respectable job as a senator's bodyguard. Many gladiators, though, were condemned criminals or slaves who were just bought to be killed in the arena. The villa owner did not expect to make money from such fighters. If they died he was not too unhappy, as it helped save on the running costs of his gladiator school.

▶ A retired gladiator teaches a youngster how to survive in the arena.

# STRIGIL

## SHAVING & BATHING

'This won't hurt ... much,' laughs the *alipila* slave as she kneels beside her master. With her sharp tweezers, she plucks unwanted hairs from his body. She then rubs warm oils on his back and scrapes away the dead skin with a strigil.

◄ A Roman strigil and oil flask.

Romans liked to bathe at public baths, but some villas also had rooms set aside for bathing and shaving. The Romans had no soap so they cleansed their skin with olive oil then scraped it with a large razor called a strigil.

*'If you do not want to make an early visit to the Underworld, then avoid Antiochus the tonsor. These scars on my chin were not caused by the sharp talons of my fierce wife but by the accursed razor of Antiochus.'* [37]

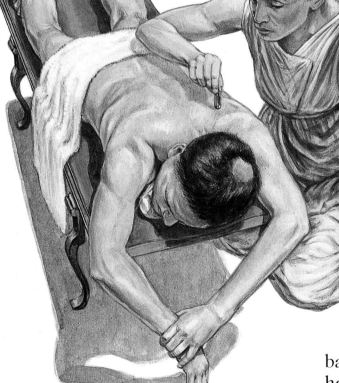

▲ A slave called the alipila, or masseuse, plucks out her master's body hair.

The Romans believed that civilized men kept their hair short. They thought that only barbarians like the Celts and Germans had long hair. One of the most important villa slaves was the *tonsor*, or barber. He had to lather, then shave, his master's head carefully every second day or so with an open steel razor.

There was usually an exercise room next door to the villa baths. Here the family relaxed, told jokes and stories, played dice or took some exercise.

*'It is important that there is a bathhouse next to the villa, so that the whole family can bathe, but only on holidays, for too much bathing makes the body weak.'* 39

*'Scrape yourself often with the curved strigil and the launderers will not wear out your towels so quickly.'* 38

◄ Women wore bikinis when bathing.

► This bath mosaic shows a lobster fighting with a squid.

Baths were decorated with mosaics showing underwater scenes. The lavish decoration of the baths was yet another way for a family to show off its wealth to the many guests.

◄ A woman exercises with dumb-bells before taking a bath.

*'How many slaves does a Roman keep? How many acres of land does he have on his villa estate? How splendid are the rooms in his villa? How relaxing are his dining couches and his baths? How numerous and how magnificent are the dishes at his banquets there? That is how the wealth of a Roman is judged.'* 40

# GLOSSARY

**ammonia**  A chemical used in preparing cloth.
**amphitheatres**  Round, open stadiums where contests were held.
**barbarian**  Rough or uncultured.
**colonnade**  A row of columns supporting a roof.
**incense**  A spice which smells sweet when it is burned.
**legions**  Divisions of the Roman army.
**masseuse**  A woman who gives massages.
**Minotaur**  A monster with a bull's head and a man's body.
**mosaic**  A picture created from small pieces of glass or stone.
**pantries**  Storerooms where food or tableware are kept.
**resplendent**  Brilliant or dazzlingly bright.
**senator**  A member of the Senate, the Roman form of parliament.
**sesterces**  Roman coins. You could buy a slave for 12,000 sesterces.
**shrine**  An alcove containing the statue of a god.
**skillet**  A small, metal cooking pot.
**sulphur**  A substance that makes a terrible smell when it is burned.
**treadwheel**  A wheel creating power from people treading on steps inside it.
**trident**  A weapon shaped like a fork with three prongs.

## SLAVES

**alipila**  A slave with skills in massage and skin-care.
**atriensis**  The keeper of the main doorway into the villa house.
**calamistera**  A slave with hairdressing skills.
**cellarius**  He was in charge of the villa pantries and cellars.
**cestellatrix**  A chamber maid who helped her mistress get dressed.
**cubicularii**  Slaves who worked in the main house on the villa estate.
**focarius**  He kept the villa's fires and ovens alight.
**lanista**  A retired gladiator who trained new fighters.
**paedagogus**  The slave in charge of the master's children.
**praegustator**  A trusted slave who tasted the master's food for poison.
**scissor**  A kitchen slave with skills in carving meat.
**scurra**  A slave who flattered his master's guests at banquets.
**silentarius**  He made sure slaves were silent in the master's presence.
**tonsor**  The slave who worked as the villa barber.

# FURTHER READING

## BOOKS TO READ

*A Traveller's Guide to Ancient Rome* by John Malam (Marshall, 1998)

*Clothes and Crafts in Roman Times* by Philip Steele (Zoe Books, 1997)

*My World – Ancient Rome* by Peter Chrisp (Franklin Watts, 1997)

*Roman Aromas* by Mary Dobson (Oxford University Press, 1997)

## SOURCES OF QUOTES

The quotes in this book are taken from the following sources:

1. *Satyricon* by Petronius Arbiter, first century AD.
2. *On Agriculture* by Lucius Iunius Columella, first century AD.
3. A letter by the Roman writer Pliny the Younger, about AD 100.
4. *On Agriculture*.
5. *On Agriculture*.
6. *On Agriculture*.
7. *Moral Epistles*, letters written by Seneca, about AD 55.
8. *About Architecture* by Vitruvius Pollio, about AD 20.
9. *On Agriculture*.
10. *Fasti*, a sacred calendar poem by the writer Ovid 43 BC–AD 17.
11. *Fasti*.
12. An essay about Roman women by Suetonius (about AD 69–130).
13. *Moral Epistles*.
14. A letter from about AD 105, by Pliny.
15. *Epigrams*, a book of sayings by the writer Martial written after AD 86.
16. *Geography* by the Greek scholar Strabo, about AD 15.
17. *On Agriculture*.
18. *On Agriculture*.
19. *On Agriculture*.
20. *On Agriculture*.
21. *Satyricon*.
22. *On Agriculture*.
23. Graffitti scratched on the wall of a kitchen in Pompeii.
24. A letter by the writer Cicero, about 62 BC.
25. *Satyricon*.
26. A note from about AD 110 by Suetonius.
27. *Moral Epistles*.
28. A fragment from an anonymous first-century Roman comedy.
29. An anonymous third-century letter.
30. A letter written about AD 100 by Pliny the Younger.
31. *Life of Cato the Elder* by Plutarch, about AD 110.
32. *Institutes of Oratory*, a book on public speaking by Quintilian, about AD 88.
33. *Epigrams*.
34. A law published in Rome in AD 121.
35. An anonymous, second-century book of sayings.
36. *Moral Epistles*.
37. *Epigrams*.
38. *Epigrams*.
39. *On Agriculture*.
40. An essay of about AD 106 by Juvenal, condemning the wealth of the rich.

# INDEX

Numbers in **bold** refer to pictures and captions.

amphorae 16, **16**, 19
animals 6, **6**, **7**, 8, **9**, 11, **11**, 15, **27**, **29**

banquets 13, 18, 20, 21, 22, 23, 29
baths 8, 28, **28**, 29, **29**

children 17, 24, **24**, 25, **25**
clothes 7, **7**, 12, 14, **14**, 15, **15**, 21, 25

decoration 8, **8**, 9, **9**

education 5, 23, 24, 25
estate 5, **5**, 7, 15, 16, **16**, **19**, 26, 29

farming 5, 15, 16, **16**, 17
food and drink 6, 7, 10, 11, 16, 17, 18, **18**, 19, **19**, 20, **20**, 21, 23

games 12, 26, 27, **27**
gardens 4, 7, 9, 23
gladiators 26, **26**, 27, **27**

hairstyles 12, **12**, 13, **13**, 15, 28
health 14, 19

jewellery 12, **12**, 13, **13**, **15**, **19**, 25, **25**

keys 6, **6**

lares and penates 10, **10**, 11, **11**
laundry 14, 29

make-up 12, 13
mirrors 8, 12, **12**
mosaics **5**, 8, **8**, 9, **9**, **19**, **27**, 29, **29**
music 20, 22, **22**, 23, **23**

poetry 23, **23**
Pompeii **8**, 9, **11**, 22
puppets 24, **24**

religion 8, 10, 11, 17, 22, 25
Roman Empire 4, 13, 15, 17
Rome 4, 5, 26

scrubbing brushes 14, **14**
skillet 18, **18**
slaves 5, **5**, 6, **6**, 7, **7**, 10, 12, **12**, 13, 14, **14**, 15, 16, **16**, 17, **17**, 18, **18**, 19, 20, **20**, 21, **21**, 22, 23, **23**, 24, **24**, 26, 27, 28, **28**, 29
strigils 28, **28**, 29

wine 6, 16, **16**, 17, **17**, 20